COME FOLLOW ME FOR TEENS

2024 STUDY GUIDE & ACTIVITY BOOK

AGES 11-18

THE BOOK OF MORMON

TWO PAGES FOR EVERY WEEKLY LESSON

ABOUT THIS BOOK

This is an activity book for tweens & teens ages 11-18. There are two pages to complete that go along with the Come, Follow Me lesson each week.

THIS BOOK BELONGS TO:

_____

LESSON SCHEDULE

January

Jan 1-7	Intro Pages
Jan 8-14	1 Nephi 1-5
Jan 15-21	1 Nephi 6-10
Jan 22-28	1 Nephi 11-15

February

Jan 29-Feb 4	1 Nephi 16-22
Feb 5-11	2 Nephi 1-2
Feb 12-18	2 Nephi 3-5
Feb 19-25	2 Nephi 6-10

March

Feb 26-Mar 3	2 Nephi 11-19
Mar 4-10	2 Nephi 20-25
Mar 11-17	2 Nephi 26-30
Mar 18-24	2 Nephi 31-33
Mar 25-31	Easter

April

April 1-7	Jacob 1-4
April 8-14	Jacob 5-7
April 15-21	Enos-Words Mormon
April 22-28	Mosiah 1-3

May

April 29-May 5	Mosiah 4-6
May 6-12	Mosiah 7-10
May 13-19	Mosiah 11-17
May 20-26	Mosiah 18-24

June

May 27-Jun 2	Mosiah 25-28
Jun 3-9	Mosiah 29-Alma 4
Jun 10-16	Alma 5-7
Jun 17-23	Alma 8-12
Jun 24-30	Alma 13-16

July

Jul 1-7	Alma 17-22
Jul 8-14	Alma 23-29
Jul 15-21	Alma 30-31
Jul 22-28	Alma 32-35

August

Jul 29-Aug 4	Alma 36-38
Aug 5-11	Alma 39-42
Aug 12-18	Alma 43-52
Aug 19-25	Alma 53-63

September

Aug 26-Sept 1	Helaman 1-6
Sept 2-8	Helaman 7-12
Sept 9-15	Helaman 13-16
Sept 16-22	3 Nephi 1-7
Sept 23-29	3 Nephi 8-11

October

Sept 30-Oct 6	3 Nephi 12-16
Oct 7-13	3 Nephi 17-19
Oct 14-20	3 Nephi 20-26
Oct 21-27	3 Nephi 27-4 Nephi

November

Oct 28-Nov 3	Mormon 1-6
Nov 4-10	Mormon 7-9
Nov 11-17	Ether 1-5
Nov 18-24	Ether 6-11

December

Nov 25-Dec 1	Ether 12-15
Dec 2-8	Moroni 1-6
Dec 9-15	Moroni 7-9
Dec 16-22	Moroni 10
Dec 23-29	Christmas

MY GOALS FOR THIS YEAR

Write or draw your spiritual, physical, social, and intellectual goals for this year below.

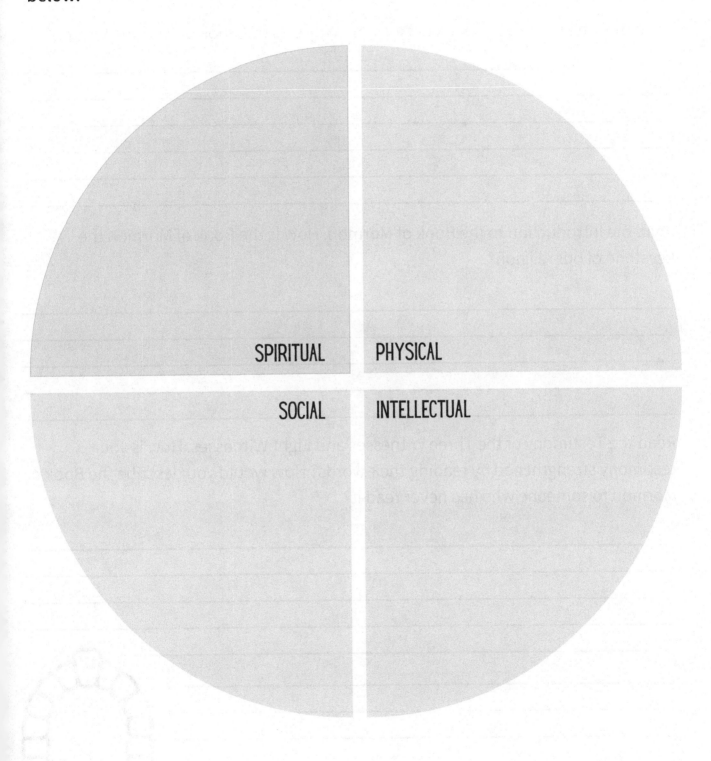

SPIRITUAL

PHYSICAL

SOCIAL

INTELLECTUAL

JANUARY 1-7

Read the Title Page of the Book of Mormon. Why was the Book of Mormon written?

_____

_____

_____

_____

_____

Read the Introduction to the Book of Mormon. How is the Book of Mormon the keystone of our religion?

_____

_____

_____

_____

_____

Read the Testimony of the Three Witnesses and Eight Witnesses. How is your testimony strengthened by reading their words? How would you describe the Book of Mormon to someone who has never read it?

_____

_____

_____

_____

_____

_____

_____

_____

INTRODUCTORY PAGES OF THE BOOK OF MORMON

Read the Testimony of the Prophet Joseph Smith. Summarize how we now have the Book of Mormon.

_____
_____
_____
_____
_____
_____
_____
_____

Write your study plan for reading the Book of Mormon this year. When and how will you study? Do you have specific things you are looking for in your study?

_____
_____
_____
_____

Write any notes and/or thoughts about this week's reading below.

_____
_____
_____
_____
_____
_____
_____
_____

JANUARY 8-14

Read 1 Nephi chapter 2. Why did Nephi have such great faith but Laman & Lemuel did not? Read 1 Nephi 15:2-11. What do these verses teach you about gaining your own testimony?

_____

_____

_____

_____

_____

Read 1 Nephi chapters 3 & 4. Why did Lehi want to get the plates of brass? How did Nephi get the plates? What do you learn from these chapters?

_____

_____

_____

_____

_____

_____

_____

_____

_____

_____

Do you ever murmur when asked to do something, such as getting up early for a service project, helping a parent, etc.? How can remembering the miracles & works of God help us stay faithful? See 1 Nephi 4:1-3; 5:1-8.

_____

_____

_____

_____

1 NEPHI 1-5

Write what you learn about each of the following people in this week's reading below.

LEHI	SARIAH	NEPHI	LAMAN & LEMUEL

Write any notes and/or thoughts about this week's reading below.

_____

_____

_____

_____

_____

_____

_____

_____

JANUARY 15-21

Heavenly Father gave Lehi a dream to teach Lehi and his family how to gain happiness. Each of the objects in the dream had a special meaning. Read 1 Nephi chapter 8 to learn about the dream. Match the object with its meaning below.

STRAIGHT & NARROW PATH

RIVER & FOUNTAIN

TREE OF LIFE

FRUIT OF THE TREE

IRON ROD

MISTS OF DARKNESS

GREAT & SPACIOUS BUILDING

LARGE & SPACIOUS FIELD

THE WORLD

BLESSINGS THAT COME THROUGH THE SAVIOR'S ATONEMENT

SATAN'S INFLUENCE IN WORLD/DEPTHS OF HELL

WORD OF GOD

OBEDIENCE TO THE COMMANDEMENTS OF GOD

TEMPTATIONS OF SATAN

PRIDEFUL& UNKIND PEOPLE WHO MOCK OTHERS

LOVE OF GOD

1 NEPHI 6-10

Read 1 Nephi 8:21-33. Write about the four groups of people below.

GROUP 1 (VS 21-23)   **GROUP 2 (VS 24-28)**   **GROUP 3 (VS 30)**   **GROUP 4 (VS 31-33)**

What differences do you notice between the four groups of people below?

_____
_____
_____
_____
_____

Read 1 Nephi chapter 10. What truths do you learn?

_____
_____
_____
_____

Write any notes and/or thoughts about this week's reading below.

_____
_____
_____
_____
_____
_____
_____
_____
_____
_____

JANUARY 22-28

Read 1 Nephi chapter 11. What did Nephi see in the vision? How does what he saw show God's great love for us?

_____

_____

_____

_____

_____

_____

Read 1 Nephi chapter 12. What did Nephi say happens to the Nephites and Lamanites in the future? Why do you think he was shown this?

_____

_____

_____

_____

_____

Read 1 Nephi 13:1-9. What is the great and abominable church?

_____

_____

_____

_____

_____

Read 1 Nephi 13:22-42. What do we learn happened to the bible over time?

_____

_____

_____

_____

_____

1 NEPHI 11-15

Read 1 Nephi 15:1-11. Why couldn't Laman & Lemuel understand the things Lehi told them? What advice did Nephi give his brothers?

_____

_____

_____

_____

_____

Read 1 Nephi 15:23–25. How does holding onto the iron rod protect you from the tempting of Satan?

_____

_____

_____

_____

_____

Write any notes and/or thoughts about this week's reading below.

_____

_____

_____

_____

_____

_____

_____

_____

_____

_____

JANUARY 29-FEBRUARY 4

Read 1 Nephi chapter 16. How are the Liahona and the Holy Ghost similar?

_____

_____

_____

_____

_____

_____

In 1 Nephi 17:7–19; 18:1–4, the Lord commands Nephi to build a boat for his family to sail to the promised land. Nephi had never done this before, so he relied on the Lord. How can we show the same faith in God as Nephi did? Would you have built a boat if you were asked or would you have said, "I can't"? Fill out the chart below with things the Lord asks of you & what you could do to get started working on it or continue working on it.

THINGS THE LORD HAS ASKED ME TO DO: WHAT I CAN DO TO GET STARTED WITH TASK:

HEAVENLY FATHER HELPS ME WITH HARD THINGS!

1 NEPHI 16-22

Nephi writes many of Isaiah's teachings. Nephi teaches that it is important to liken scriptures to ourselves. Why is that? See 1 Nephi 19:22-24.

_____
_____
_____
_____
_____
_____

How could you liken 1 Nephi 20:17-22 to yourself?

_____
_____
_____
_____
_____

Write any notes and/or thoughts about this week's reading below.

_____
_____
_____
_____
_____
_____
_____
_____
_____
_____
_____
_____

FEBRUARY 5-11

CIRCLE THE DAYS YOU READ THIS WEEK: MON TUES WED THUR FRI SAT SUN

In 2 Nephi 2:11, 16, 27, Lehi teaches his family that there must be opposition in all things. Why must there be opposition in life?

_____

_____

_____

_____

_____

Why was the fall of Adam so important? See 2 Nephi 2:17-26. What would have happened if Adam & Eve hadn't partaken of the forbidden fruit?

_____

_____

_____

_____

_____

_____

_____

Write any notes and/or thoughts about this week's reading below.

_____

_____

_____

_____

_____

_____

_____

_____

_____

2 NEPHI 1-2

In 2 Nephi 2, Lehi teaches that Adam and Eve partaking of the forbidden fruit made it possible for all of us on Earth to have the gift of agency. We can choose good or evil. Crack the code to find a message from this week's lesson.

CRACK THE CODE

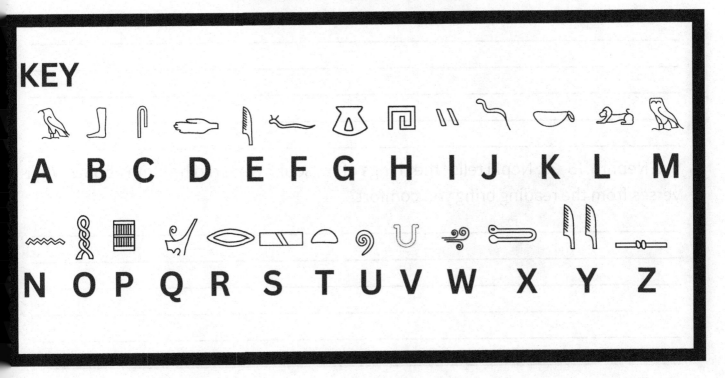

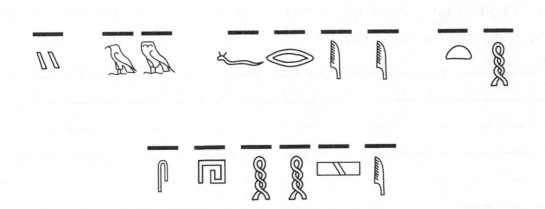

FEBRUARY 12-18

In 2 Nephi 3:6, we learn about a "choice seer," who we now know was Joseph Smith. A seer is someone who has the gift from God of being able to see spiritually. What do we learn in chapter 3 about how Joseph Smith would bless God's children?

_____

_____

_____

_____

_____

_____

_____

In 2 Nephi 4:15–35, Nephi tells "the things of his soul." What did he write about? What verses from the reading bring you comfort?

_____

_____

_____

_____

_____

_____

_____

Read 2 Nephi 5:16-34. What curse came upon the Lamanites? Write any notes and/or thoughts about this week's reading below.

_____

_____

_____

_____

_____

_____

2 NEPHI 3-5

In 2 Nephi 5:15–16, Nephi builds a temple. What is special about temples? In the box below, draw a picture of what you think Nephi's temple looked like.

TEMPLES ARE HOUSES OF THE LORD

FEBRUARY 19-25

Read 2 Nephi 6:4-5. Why do Nephi and Jacob quote Isaiah so often?

_____

_____

_____

_____

_____

Read 2 Nephi 9:1-25. What would happen to us without the Atonement?

_____

_____

_____

_____

_____

Read 2 Nephi 9:26-54. What warnings & invitations does Jacob give us in these verses?

_____

_____

_____

_____

_____

Write any notes and/or thoughts about this week's reading below.

_____

_____

_____

_____

_____

2 NEPHI 6-10

In 2 Nephi 9:49, we learn to let our hearts "delight" in righteousness and praise God. In the hearts below, write good "righteous" choices you can make.

"MY HEART DELIGHTETH IN RIGHTEOUSNESS"

FEBRUARY 26-MARCH 3

Read 2 Nephi 11:2-4. Why did Nephi write down the words of Isaiah?

_____

_____

_____

_____

_____

Read 2 Nephi 12:2-3. Why do you think a mountain is a good symbol for the temple?

_____

_____

_____

_____

_____

Read 2 Nephi 15:20. Why does Satan like to make evil things look good?

_____

_____

_____

_____

_____

Write any notes and/or thoughts about this week's reading below.

_____

_____

_____

_____

_____

_____

2 NEPHI 11-19

Throughout the scriptures, many names are given to Jesus. In 2 Nephi 11:4–7; 17:14; 19:6, some of those names are listed. Color the names of Christ below and discuss with your family or class what those names mean.

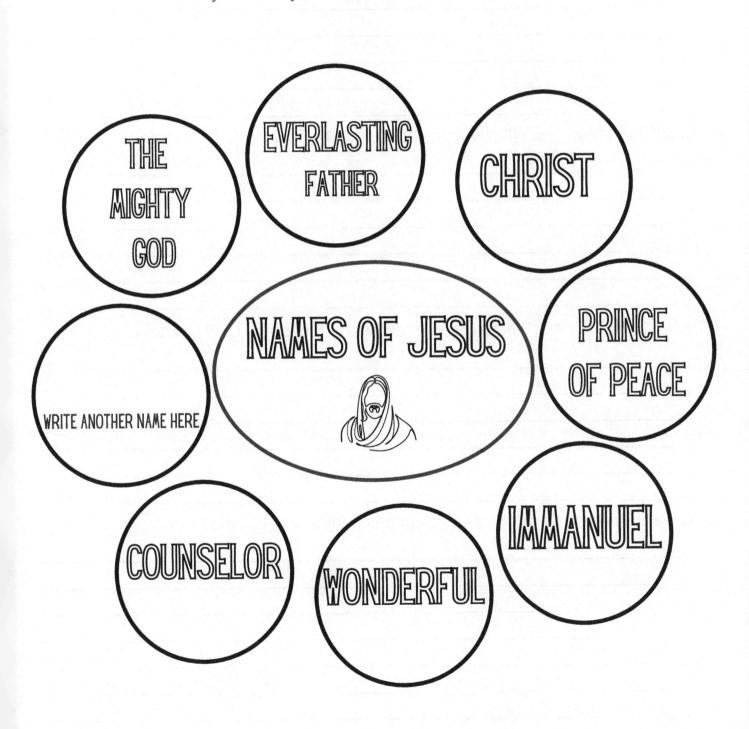

MARCH 4-10

What do the cities listed in 2 Nephi 20:9-11 have in common?

_____

_____

_____

_____

_____

Read 2 Nephi 21:6–9. What will the millennium be like?

_____

_____

_____

_____

_____

Read 2 Nephi 22:4-5. What are some "excellent things" the Lord has done?

_____

_____

_____

_____

_____

Write any notes and/or thoughts about this week's reading below.

_____

_____

_____

_____

_____

2 NEPHI 20-25

In 2 Nephi 21:11–12, we learn the Lord is gathering His people and setting up an "ensign for the nations." On the flag below, draw pictures and and write words to represent your testimony & what you love about the Gospel of Christ.

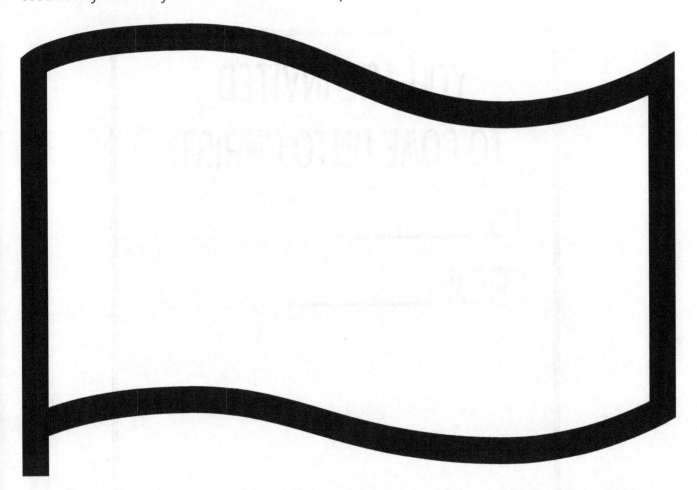

In 2 Nephi 25:26, we learn about "rejoicing" in Christ. Fill in the missing words in the scripture below and see if you can memorize the scripture.

"AND WE _____ OF CHRIST, WE _____ IN CHRIST, WE _____ OF CHRIST, WE _____ OF CHRIST, AND WE WRITE ACCORDING TO OUR PROPHECIES, THAT OUR _____ MAY KNOW TO WHAT SOURCE THEY MAY LOOK FOR A REMISSION OF THEIR _____"

MARCH 11-17

In 2 Nephi 26:23–28, 33, Jesus invites everyone to come unto Him and partake of His goodness and salvation. Think of someone you could invite to "come unto Christ" and decorate and fill out the invite below and decorate.

YOU ARE INVITED
TO COME UNTO CHRIST!

TO: _____

FROM: _____

Read chapter 27. What are some things that will happen in the last days?

_____

_____

_____

_____

_____

Read chapter 28. List lies Satan uses to deceive taught in this chapter.

_____

_____

_____

_____

_____

In 2 Nephi 28:2, we learn the Book of Mormon is of "great worth" to us. Why is the Book of Mormon important to you?

_____

_____

_____

_____

Write any notes and/or thoughts about this week's reading below.

_____

_____

_____

_____

_____

_____

MARCH 18-24

In 2 Nephi 31, Nephi tells us the steps we need to take to receive eternal life. Write or draw some of the steps below on the stepping stones. Some examples include being baptized, receiving the Holy Ghost, keeping the commandments, repenting, etc.

STEPS TO ETERNAL LIFE

2 NEPHI 31-33

Read 2 Nephi 31:4-8. Why was Christ baptized?

_____

_____

_____

_____

_____

Read 2 Nephi 33:3-5. How do you think prophets feel about their people?

_____

_____

_____

_____

_____

Read 2 Nephi 33:11. Does the Book of Mormon contain Christ's words? How do you know?

_____

_____

_____

_____

Write any notes and/or thoughts about this week's reading below.

_____

_____

_____

_____

_____

_____

_____

MARCH 25-31

Read 2 Nephi 9:6-15, 22. What do you learn about the resurrection in these verses?

_____

_____

_____

_____

_____

Read Alma 7:11-13. What did the Savior suffer? Why? What does this mean to you?

_____

_____

_____

_____

_____

Read Mosiah 27:8-28. How can the Savior change you?

_____

_____

_____

_____

_____

Write any notes and/or thoughts about this week's reading below.

_____

_____

_____

_____

_____

EASTER

Read Matthew chapters 21, 26-28. Match the correct words with the correct picture to learn about the final week's life of Christ's life.

PALM SUNDAY - JOYFUL ENTRANCE TO JERUSALEM

MONDAY - JESUS CLEANSES THE TEMPLE

TUESDAY & WEDNESDAY - TEACHING IN JERUSALEM

THURSDAY - PASSOVER & ORDINANCE OF SACRAMENT

THURSDAY - GARDEN OF GETHSEMANE

FRIDAY - JESUS IS CRUCIFIED

SATURDAY - CHRIST'S BODY IN THE TOMB

SUNDAY - JESUS CHRIST IS RESURRECTED & APPEARS TO MARY & APOSTLES

APRIL 1-7

CIRCLE THE DAYS YOU READ THIS WEEK: MON TUES WED THUR FRI SAT SUN

Read Jacob 1:19. What does it mean to "magnify our office"?

_____

_____

_____

_____

_____

Read Jacob 2:13. Why must we be cautious of the love of wealth?

_____

_____

_____

_____

_____

Read Jacob 2:22-35. What were some of the "grosser" crimes in Jacob's day?

_____

_____

_____

_____

Read Jacob 3:3-10. How were the Lamanites more righteous at this time than the Nephites?

_____

_____

_____

_____

_____

JACOB 1-4

Read Jacob 4:5. What was the purpose of the law of Moses?

_____

_____

_____

_____

_____

Read Jacob 4:14-18. What can we do to avoid spiritual blindness?

_____

_____

_____

_____

_____

Write any notes and/or thoughts about this week's reading below.

_____

_____

_____

_____

_____

_____

_____

_____

_____

_____

_____

_____

_____

APRIL 8-14

In Jacob chapter 5, we learn of the allegory of the Olive Tree, which represents the Lord's dealings with the House of Israel and the Gentiles. As you read the chapter with your family or class, match the symbol to it's meaning.

LORD OF THE VINEYARD

VINEYARD

SERVANTS

TAME OLIVE TREE

WILD OLIVE TREE

GOOD & BAD FRUIT

DECAY

GRAFTING

PRUNING, DIGGING, DUNGING

BURNING THE VINEYARD

PROPHETS

GENTILES/THOSE WHO HAVEN'T MADE COVENANTS WITH THE LORD

WORKS OF MEN

JOINING THE HOUSE OF ISRAEL

NOURISHING OTHERS TO RECEIVE BLESSINGS OF SALVATION

JESUS CHRIST

THE WORLD

HOUSE OF ISRAEL/GOD'S COVENANT PEOPLE

APOSTASY & WICKEDNESS

END OF THE WORLD/JUDGEMENT OF GOD

JACOB 5-7

Read Jacob 5:4. Why does the Lord want to care for a tree that is decaying?

_____

_____

_____

_____

_____

Read Jacob 5:32. Why does it grieve the Lord that he should lose a tree? What does that phrase reveal?

_____

_____

_____

_____

Read Jacob chapter 7. What do you learn from the story of Sherem?

_____

_____

_____

_____

Write any notes and/or thoughts about this week's reading below.

_____

_____

_____

_____

_____

_____

_____

APRIL 15-21

In Enos, we read about him going out to hunt in the forest and praying to God. He prayed for himself, his brethren the Nephites, and the Lamanites. In the bubbles below, draw or write things you could pray for. Think about Enos and how he prayed not only for himself, but for others.

THINGS I CAN PRAY FOR

ENOS-WORDS OF MORMON

Read Enos 1:1-18. What can you learn from Enos about prayer?

_____

_____

_____

_____

Read Enos 1:19-24. Describe the Nephites and Lamanites in Enos' day.

_____

_____

_____

_____

Read Omni. Why was so little written by the first few authors of the book of Omni?

_____

_____

_____

_____

Write any notes and/or thoughts about this week's reading below.

_____

_____

_____

_____

_____

_____

APRIL 22-28

In Mosiah 2:17, King Benjamin teaches the importance of serving others. When we serve others, we are serving God. Fill in the missing words from this important scripture verse below.

AND BEHOLD, I TELL YOU THESE THINGS THAT YE MAY LEARN _____; THAT YE MAY _____ THAT WHEN YE ARE IN THE _____ OF YOUR _____ BEINGS YE ARE _____ IN THE SERVICE OF YOUR _____.

Can you think of someone you could serve this week? Write who you can serve and what you will do below.

_____
_____
_____
_____

Service recap: Once your service is completed, write how it went and how you felt below.

_____
_____
_____
_____
_____
_____

MOSIAH 1-3

Read Mosiah 2:1-20. What do you learn about serving from King Benjamin?

_____
_____
_____
_____
_____

Read Mosiah 2:31-41. Why does happiness come from keeping God's commandments?

_____
_____
_____
_____
_____

Read Mosiah 3:1-13. What do you learn about the Savior and His mission in these verses?

_____
_____
_____
_____
_____

Write any notes and/or thoughts about this week's reading below.

_____
_____
_____
_____
_____
_____
_____

In Mosiah 4:1–3, 10, we learn that repentance brings us joy. We can repent because of the Atonement. Color the steps of repentance below.

MOSIAH 4-6

Read Mosiah chapter 4. What inspires you from King Benjamin's address?

_____
_____
_____
_____
_____

Read Mosiah 4:16-26. What do we learn about caring for the poor in these verses?

_____
_____
_____
_____
_____

Read Mosiah 5:2. What is the "mighty change" talked about?

_____
_____
_____
_____

Write any notes and/or thoughts about this week's reading below.

_____
_____
_____
_____
_____

In Mosiah 10:10–11, we learn an important lesson. Crack the code below to get the message.

CRACK THE CODE

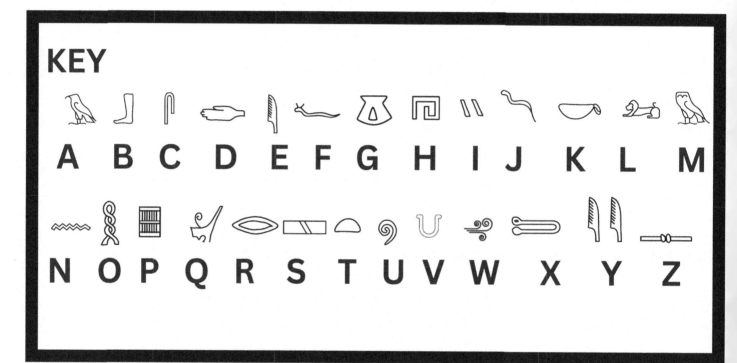

KEY

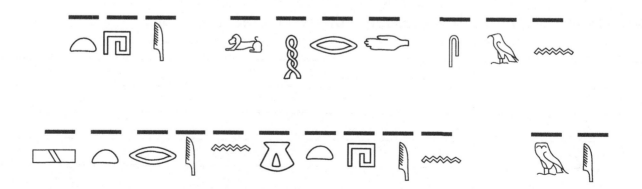

MOSIAH 7-10

Read Mosiah 8:13-21. What do you learn about seers from Ammon?

_____

_____

_____

_____

_____

Read Mosiah chapter 9. Summarize the account Zeniff gives in this chapter.

_____

_____

_____

_____

_____

_____

Read Mosiah 10:11-18. What do we learn about false traditions influencing generations?

_____

_____

_____

_____

_____

Write any notes and/or thoughts about this week's reading below.

_____

_____

_____

_____

_____

_____

MAY 13-19

Read Mosiah chapter 11. How would you describe King Noah and Abinadi?

_____

_____

_____

_____

_____

Read Mosiah chapter 12. Why was Abinadi arrested?

_____

_____

_____

_____

_____

Read Mosiah 17:11-12. Why did King Noah's priests want Abinadi slain?

_____

_____

_____

_____

_____

Write any notes and/or thoughts about this week's reading below.

_____

_____

_____

_____

_____

_____

_____

MOSIAH 11-17

In this week's reading, we learn about the courageous prophet Abinadi. As you read, match the correct passage below to the corresponding picture.

REPENT!

KING NOAH WAS A WICKED, LAZY KING

ABINADI WAS GOD'S PROPHET WHO TOLD KING NOAH AND HIS PEOPLE TO REPENT

KING NOAH'S PRIESTS TRIED TRICKING ABINADI WITH THEIR QUESTIONS, BUT THEY COULDN'T.

ALMA WAS THE ONLY KING'S PRIEST TO BELIEVE ABINADI. HE RAN AWAY AND HID SO HE WOULDN'T BE KILLED.

ABINADI WOULDN'T DENY HIS FAITH AND ALL HE HAD PREACHED, SO HE WAS BURNED.

KING NOAH'S FOLLOWERS BURNED HIM, AS ABINADI PROPHESIED. (CHAPTER 19)

MAY 20-26

Read Mosiah 18:8–10 and Doctrine and Covenants 20:37 and learn about the covenants we make when we are baptized. Fill in the blanks below with one of the words listed.

WHAT I PROMISE

I WILL FOLLOW _____

I WILL _____ OTHERS

I WILL STAND AS A _____ OF GOD

I WILL SERVE GOD & _____ HIS COMMANDMENTS

WITNESS   KEEP   JESUS   HELP

HEAVENLY FATHER PROMISES

HE WILL _____ ME

HE WILL GIVE ME THE _____ OF THE HOLY GHOST

HE WILL GIVE ME ETERNAL _____

FORGIVE   GIFT   LIFE

MOSIAH 18-24

Read Mosiah chapter 19. What do we learn about King Noah's character in this chapter?

_____
_____
_____
_____
_____

Read Mosiah chapter 22. How did Limhi and his people escape the Lamanites?

_____
_____
_____
_____
_____
_____

Read Mosiah chapter 23. Why did Alma refuse to be king?

_____
_____
_____
_____
_____

Write any notes and/or thoughts about this week's reading below.

_____
_____
_____
_____
_____
_____
_____

MAY 27-JUNE 2

CIRCLE THE DAYS YOU READ THIS WEEK: MON TUES WED THUR FRI SAT SUN

Read Mosiah 26:1-19. Why do you think the "rising generation" fell away from the church?

_____

_____

_____

_____

_____

Read 27:11-14. Why was an angel sent to Alma the younger & the sons of Mosiah?

_____

_____

_____

_____

_____

Read Mosiah 27:19-37. How was Alma the Younger spiritually reborn?

_____

_____

_____

_____

Write any notes and/or thoughts about this week's reading below.

_____

_____

_____

_____

_____

_____

MOSIAH 25-28

In Mosiah 27:8–24, we read about Alma asking his people to fast and pray for Alma the Younger. What other scripture stories can you think of where the people fasted? Is there someone you and your family could fast together for? Color the pictures below and learn more about fasting.

If you are healthy and when you feel ready, you can begin to fast.

Fast Sunday at church is usually the first Sunday of the month.

When fasting, you skip eating & drinking (usually 2 meals).

Pick something or someone to fast for and say a prayer before, during, and after fast.

The money you would have spent on meals during your fast can be given as a fast offering to help those in need.

Look for the blessings and miracles fasting brings.

JUNE 3-9

Read Mosiah 29. What are the dangers of being led by a king?

_____

_____

_____

_____

_____

Read Alma chapter 1. Why do you think the people liked what Nehor taught?

_____

_____

_____

_____

_____

Read Alma chapter 2. Who was Amlici? Summarize his actions.

_____

_____

_____

_____

Write any notes and/or thoughts about this week's reading below.

_____

_____

_____

_____

_____

_____

_____

MOSIAH 29-ALMA 4

In Alma 4:8–20, we learn that Alma stepped down as Chief Judge among the people so he could go and share his testimony with the people to help bring them back to Christ. What is a testimony? Color the foundations of a testimony below. How is growing your testimony like taking care of a garden?

GOD LIVES & LOVES ME

JESUS ATONED FOR MY SINS

THIS IS GOD'S TRUE CHURCH

THE CHURCH IS LED BY A LIVING PROPHET

A TESTIMONY IS LIKE A GARDEN

JUNE 10-16

In Alma 5:14–33, Alma asks a lot of great questions we can ask ourselves to make sure we are staying close to the Savior. Alma asks if we have had "a mighty change" in our hearts. Write in the heart below what you can do to keep close to the Savior.

I CAN HAVE A CHANGE OF HEART & STAY CLOSE TO THE SAVIOR BY:

ALMA 5-7

What stands out to you in Alma chapter 5?

_____

_____

_____

_____

_____

Read Alma chapter 6. How was the church in Zarahemla put in order?

_____

_____

_____

_____

_____

Read Alma 7:14-21. What must we do to enter the kingdom of God?

_____

_____

_____

_____

_____

Write any notes and/or thoughts about this week's reading below.

_____

_____

_____

_____

_____

_____

JUNE 17-23

In Alma 8:18–22, we learn how Amulek was a good friend to Alma. What are some things you can do to be a good friend? Write ways in the circles below. Color the two friends.

I CAN BE A GOOD FRIEND BY...

ALMA 8-12

Read Alma chapter 8. Why did the people of Ammonihah reject Alma's words?

_____
_____
_____
_____
_____
_____

Read Alma chapter 9. Why would it be more tolerable for the Lamanites to transgress than the Nephites?

_____
_____
_____
_____

What do we learn about Zeezrom in Alma 11:21-22?

_____
_____
_____
_____
_____

Write any notes and/or thoughts about this week's reading below.

_____
_____
_____
_____
_____
_____
_____

JUNE 24-30

Read Alma 14:10-13. Why did Alma not use the power of God to save the innocent being burned?

_____

_____

_____

_____

_____

Read Alma 14:23-29. How were Alma and Amulek set free?

_____

_____

_____

_____

_____

Read Alma chapter 15. What happened to Zeezrom after he was healed?

_____

_____

_____

_____

_____

Write any notes and/or thoughts about this week's reading below.

_____

_____

_____

_____

_____

_____

ALMA 13-16

In this week's reading, we learn about the righteous being burned and Alma and Amulek being freed from prison miraculously. Match each event to it's correct picture below.

WICKED PEOPLE THROW WOMEN & CHILDREN WHO BELIEVED WORD OF GOD INTO A FIRE TO DIE

ALMA AND AMULEK PUT IN PRISON

ALMA AND AMULEK TIED UP & TAKEN TO CHIEF JUDGE

PRION WALLS FELL & EVERYONE INSIDE WAS KILLED EXCEPT ALMA & AMULEK

WICKED PEOPLE IN AMMONIHAH KILLED BY LAMANITES

ZEEZROM REPENTS, IS HEALED, AND IS BAPTIZED

JULY 1-7

In this week's lesson, we learn about the sons of Mosiah going to preach the gospel to the Lamanites. Pretend you are a missionary and write or draw some things you would tell people on the doors below.

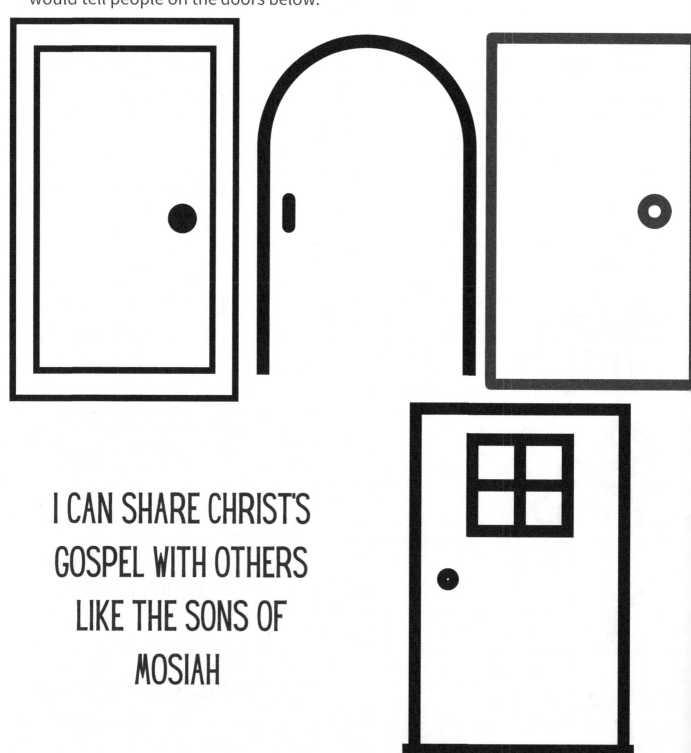

I CAN SHARE CHRIST'S GOSPEL WITH OTHERS LIKE THE SONS OF MOSIAH

ALMA 17-22

Read Alma chapter 17. Summarize the story of Ammon saving the king's sheep.

_____
_____
_____
_____
_____

Read Alma 19:16-17. Who was Abish? How was she converted to the gospel?

_____
_____
_____
_____
_____

Read Alma chapter 22. What did Aaron teach king Lamoni's father?

_____
_____
_____
_____
_____

Write any notes and/or thoughts about this week's reading below.

_____
_____
_____
_____
_____
_____
_____

JULY 8-14

In Alma 24:17-18, the Anti-Nephi-Lehies, buried all their weapons of war. They did this as a testimony to God that they would never use weapons to shed another person's blood. Color the picture below.

WHAT DO YOU LEARN ABOUT PEOPLE'S ABILITY TO CHANGE FROM THIS STORY?

_____

_____

_____

_____

_____

THE LORD BLESSES ME AS I WORK TO KEEP MY PROMISES TO HIM

ALMA 23-29

Read Alma chapter 23. Which Lamanite cities were converted to the gospel?

_____

_____

_____

_____

_____

_____

Read 25:15-16. How did the Nephites' view of the law of Moses differ from the Jews?

_____

_____

_____

_____

_____

_____

Read Alma chapter 26. How does sharing the gospel bring us joy?

_____

_____

_____

_____

_____

Write any notes and/or thoughts about this week's reading below.

_____

_____

_____

_____

_____

_____

_____

JULY 15-21

Read Alma 30:12-17. What false teachings was Korihor preaching? Do we have similar fa
teachings today?

_____

_____

_____

_____

_____

Read Alma 30:3-42. What did Alma testify to Korihor?

_____

_____

_____

_____

_____

_____

Read Alma 30:43-60. What happened to Korihor?

_____

_____

_____

_____

_____

Write any notes and/or thoughts about this week's reading below.

_____

_____

_____

_____

_____

_____

_____

_____

ALMA 30-31

In Alma 31, Alma and some missionaries went to preach to the Zoramites. The Zoramites would take turns standing on a tall tower and repeat the same prayer. Listed below the "rameumptom" on this page are some of the Zoramites false beliefs. Match the false belief with the opposite, true doctrine of Christ that Alma taught.

ZORAMITE'S BELIEFS

DOCTRINE OF CHRIST

GOD IS A SPIRIT

THERE WOULD BE NO CHRIST

ZORAMITES THOUGHT ONLY THEY WOULD BE SAVED

ZORAMITES ALL SAID THE EXACT SAME PRAYER

AFTER THEY PRAYED, THEY WENT HOME & DID NOT PRAY OR TALK OF GOD AGAIN THE REST OF THE WEEK

THEY LOVED RICHES AND WORLDLY THINGS & BRAGGED ABOUT THEIR RICHES

CHRIST WOULD COME AND ATONE FOR THE SINS OF ALL MANKIND

WE SHOULD PRAY ALWAYS & BE AN EXAMPLE OF CHRIST EVERY DAY

WE SHOULD PUT THE THINGS OF GOD FIRST

EVERYONE CAN BE SAVED THROUGH CHRIST'S ATONEMENT

GOD HAS A BODY

GOD DOESN'T WANT US TO JUST REPEAT REPETITIONS IN OUR PRAYERS, BUT TO SHARE THINGS ON OUR HEART

JULY 22-28

Read Alma 32:1-21. Why is humility important?

_____
_____
_____
_____
_____

Read Alma 32:22-43. What do you learn about faith in these verses?

_____
_____
_____
_____
_____

Read Alma chapter 33. How and where can we worship and pray?

_____
_____
_____
_____

Read Alma 34:8-16. What do you learn about the atonement in these verses?

_____
_____
_____
_____
_____
_____
_____

ALMA 32-35

Read Alma 34:30-36. Why should we not procrastinate repentance?

_____
_____
_____
_____
_____

Read Alma 35. Why were the Zoramites angry? What did they do because of their anger?

_____
_____
_____
_____
_____

Write any notes and/or thoughts about this week's reading below.

_____
_____
_____
_____
_____
_____
_____
_____
_____
_____
_____
_____

JULY 29-AUGUST 4

CIRCLE THE DAYS YOU READ THIS WEEK: MON TUES WED THUR FRI SAT SUN

ALMA'S ADVICE ON BEING A GOOD MISSIONARY

In Alma chapter 38, Alma gives advice to Shiblon about being a good missionary.
Write things he advices to do and not to do in the columns below.

THINGS TO DO: THINGS NOT TO DO:

What talents do you have that make you a good missionary now and in future?

_____

_____

_____

_____

_____

_____

ALMA 36-38

Read Alma chapter 36. What does Alma teach and testify to his son Helaman? Why does he tell his conversion story?

_____
_____
_____
_____

How was Alma finally converted? (see vs. 17-20)

_____
_____
_____
_____
_____

Read Alma 37:1-15. What small and simple things bring you closer to Christ?

_____
_____
_____
_____
_____

Write any notes and/or thoughts about this week's reading below.

_____
_____
_____
_____
_____
_____
_____

AUGUST 5-11

Read Alma 39. What do we learn from Corianton about the importance of living the law of chastity?

_____

_____

_____

_____

_____

Read Alma 40:23. What will our bodies be like after being resurrected?

_____

_____

_____

_____

_____

_____

Read Alma 42:1-15. Why was the fall of Adam so important in Heavenly Father's plan?

_____

_____

_____

_____

_____

Read Alma 42:18-30. Why is sorrow for sin an important part of repentance?

_____

_____

_____

_____

_____

_____

_____

ALMA 39-42

Write any notes and/or thoughts about this week's reading below.

_____

_____

_____

_____

_____

_____

In Alma 40, we learn more about what happens when we die. Complete the word search below with words from the reading.

```
G  P  J  U  D  G  E  M  E  N  T
T  J  S  T  B  O  D  Y  H  I  C
U  H  T  A  S  B  I  R  R  D  O
D  R  B  A  L  Q  J  I  L  J  P
P  O  H  F  O  E  P  R  Q  F  A
L  L  P  R  I  S  O  N  R  J  R
L  H  D  H  Q  W  Y  L  P  W  A
I  R  E  R  T  W  Y  F  O  I  D
V  I  A  T  L  W  W  O  T  B  I
E  D  T  C  O  O  P  D  H  R  S
M  Q  H  G  Y  S  F  B  K  N  E
```

SPIRIT	WORLD	DEATH
PARADISE	PRISON	JUDGEMENT
BODY	LIVE	

AUGUST 12-18

CIRCLE THE DAYS YOU READ THIS WEEK: MON TUES WED THUR FRI SAT SUN

Read Alma 44:1-7. How did Captain Moroni offer peace to Zerahemnah? Why did Zerahemnah refuse?

_____

_____

_____

_____

_____

Read Alma 46:11-18. Why did Captain Moroni make a title of liberty?

_____

_____

_____

_____

_____

_____

Read Alma chapter 47. How did Amalickiah use deception to gain control of the Lamanite kingdom?

_____

_____

_____

_____

_____

Write any notes and/or thoughts about this week's reading below.

_____

_____

_____

_____

_____

_____

_____

In Alma 48:7–9, we learn some of the ways the Nephites fortified their cities. How can we fortify and protect our homes spiritually against Satan? Write the ways in the home below.

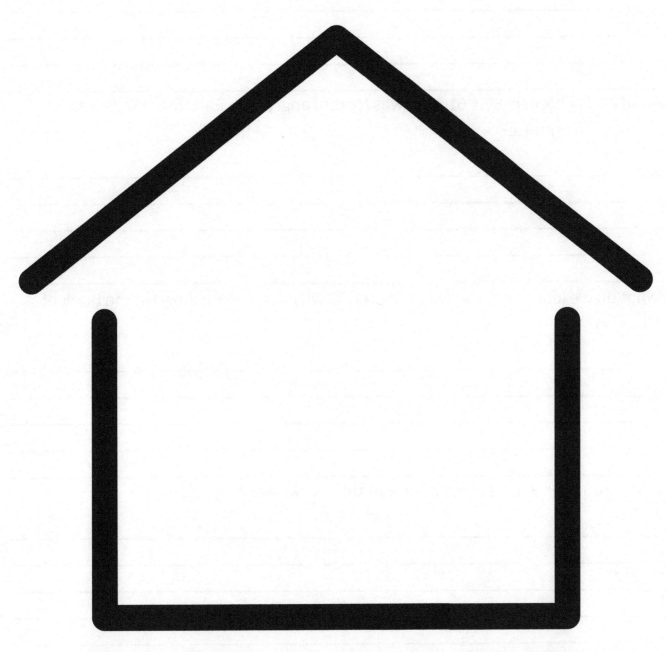

WE CAN SPIRITUALLY PROTECT OUR HOMES

AUGUST 19-25

Read Alma 53:20-21. What were some of the qualities of the stripling warriors? Read Alma chapter 57. What do we learn from the stripling warriors being miraculously preserved?

_____

_____

_____

_____

Read Alma chapters 60 & 61. Why was Moroni angry with Pahoran? What was Pahoran's response?

_____

_____

_____

_____

What do we learn from the "war chapters"? Why are they included in the Book of Mormon?

_____

_____

_____

_____

Write any notes and/or thoughts about this week's reading below.

_____

_____

_____

_____

_____

_____

_____

In Alma 56:48, we learn what the Army of Helaman soldiers said about their mothers. Crack the code below to read their message.

CRACK THE CODE

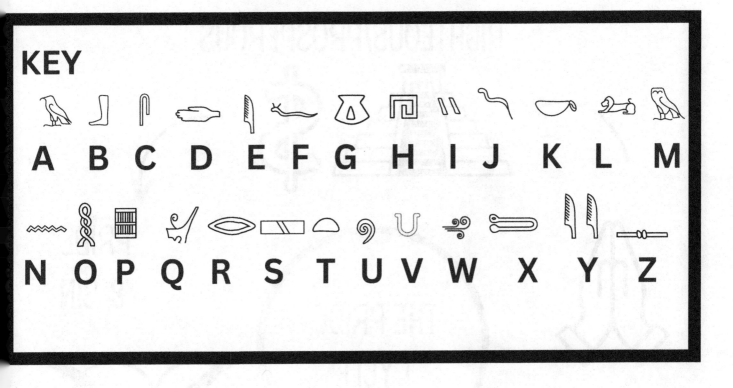

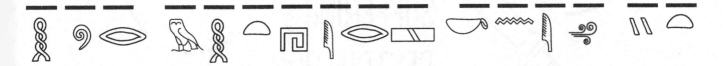

In Helaman 3:24, 33–34; 4:11–15, we see a pattern that is shown throughout the Book of Mormon called the "Pride Cycle." The people are righteous and begin to prosper and then pride and sin creeps in and they make choices that causes suffering and destruction. They then repent and humble themselves and become a righteous people again. Color the pictures below of the pride cycle.

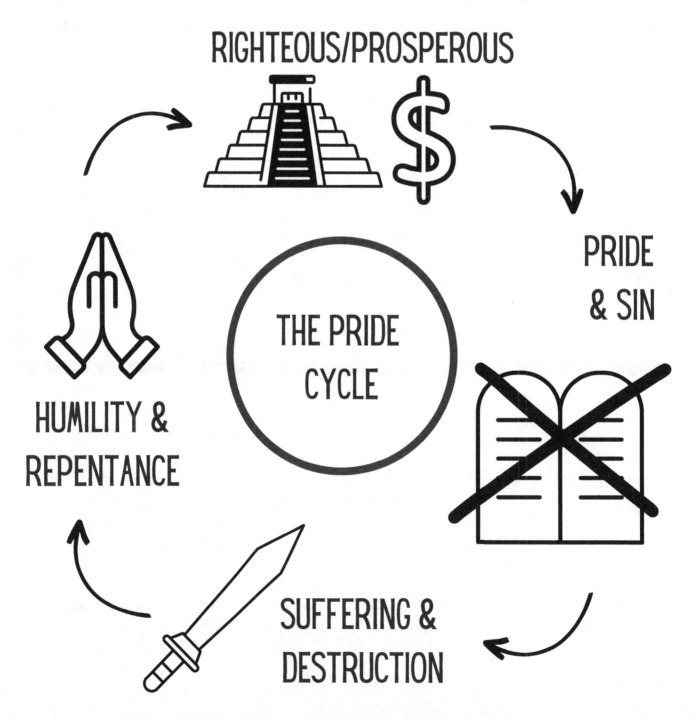

HELAMAN 1-6

Read Helaman chapter 2. What happened to Kishkumen?

_____

_____

_____

_____

_____

Read Helaman 3:24-32 & 33-34. What differences do you see in the people in these verses?

_____

_____

_____

_____

_____

How were Nephi & Lehi miraculously saved from prison?

_____

_____

_____

_____

_____

Write any notes and/or thoughts about this week's reading below.

_____

_____

_____

_____

_____

_____

_____

SEPTEMBER 2-8

Read Helaman chapter 7. How can wickedness occur so quickly in a society?

_____

_____

_____

_____

_____

See Helaman 925-41. What did Nephi tell the people to do to reveal that Seantum murdered Seezoram?

_____

_____

_____

_____

_____

Read Helaman chapter 11. Why does it oftentimes take extremes to convince the people to repent?

_____

_____

_____

_____

_____

Write any notes and/or thoughts about this week's reading below.

_____

_____

_____

_____

_____

_____

_____

HELAMAN 7-12

In Helaman 8:13–23, we are reminded of the many prophets who testified of Christ. The prophet leads us to Jesus. On the foot prints below, write ways prophets help you come unto Christ.

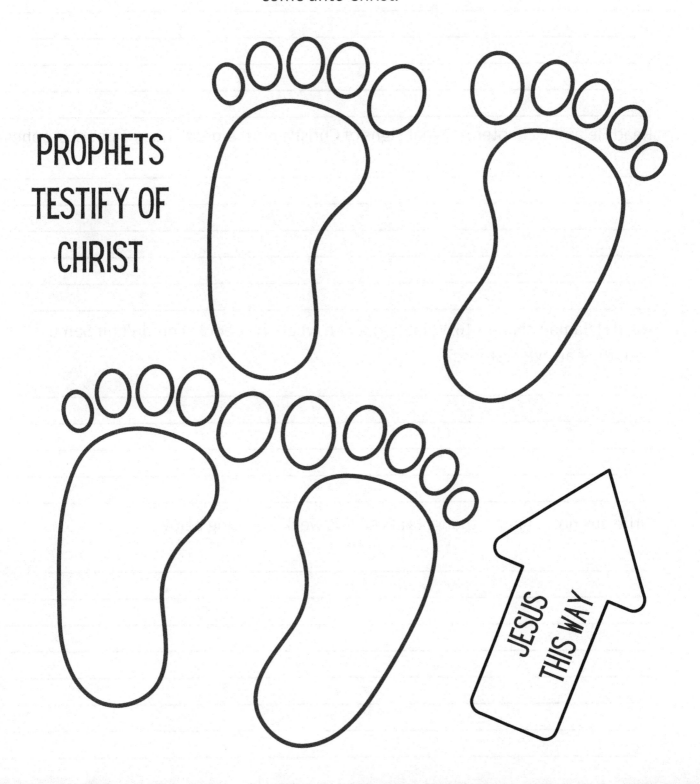

PROPHETS
TESTIFY OF
CHRIST

JESUS
THIS WAY

SEPTEMBER 9-15

CIRCLE THE DAYS YOU READ THIS WEEK: MON TUES WED THUR FRI SAT SUN

Read Helaman 13:24-30. Why are living prophets often rejected?

_____

_____

_____

_____

_____

Read Helaman chapter 14. What signs of Christ's birth & death does Samuel prophesy?

_____

_____

_____

_____

_____

Read Helaman chapter 16. What happened when the people couldn't hit Samuel with their arrows & stones?

_____

_____

_____

_____

Write any notes and/or thoughts about this week's reading below.

_____

_____

_____

_____

_____

_____

_____

HELAMAN 13-16

In Helaman 13:2–5, we learn that Samuel spoke the things that God put in his heart. God speaks to us through the Holy Ghost. Color the ways below that the Holy Ghost can communicate God's message to us.

THOUGHTS THAT STAY ON YOUR MIND

SOMETHING YOU FEEL IN YOUR HEART

A WHISPER OR VOICE YOU HEAR IN YOUR MIND

A FEELING THAT YOU SHOULDN'T DO SOMETHING

A DESIRE TO FOLLOW THE COMMANDMENTS

A HAPPY, PEACEFUL FEELING THAT SOMETHING IS A GOOD CHOICE

GOD CAN SPEAK TO ME THROUGH THE HOLY GHOST

SEPTEMBER 16-22

In 3 Nephi 1:4–15, 19–21, we read that the sign was given that Christ was born. There was a night without darkness and a new star appeared. Color the picture below and list other signs that were given of Christ's birth.

OTHER SIGNS GIVEN:

THE NEPHITES SAW A NEW STAR APPEAR WHEN JESUS WAS BORN

3 NEPHI 1-7

Read 3 Nephi 1:9-15. What did God tell Nephi when he prayed for the believers who were to be put to death?

_____

_____

_____

_____

Read 3 Nephi chapter 3. What can we learn from the example of Lachoneus?

_____

_____

_____

_____

_____

Read 3 Nephi chapter 4. What lesson can we learn from the Nephites about being prepared?

_____

_____

_____

_____

Write any notes and/or thoughts about this week's reading below.

_____

_____

_____

_____

_____

_____

_____

SEPTEMBER 23-29

CIRCLE THE DAYS YOU READ THIS WEEK: MON TUES WED THUR FRI SAT SUN

Read 3 Nephi chapter 8. What events occurred to attest the crucifixion of Christ?

_____

_____

_____

_____

_____

Read 3 Nephi chapter 9. What did the voice of Christ proclaim in this chapter?

_____

_____

_____

_____

_____

Read 3 Nephi chapter 11:18-30. What did Christ teach about baptism?

_____

_____

_____

_____

_____

Write any notes and/or thoughts about this week's reading below.

_____

_____

_____

_____

_____

_____

_____

_____

In 3 Nephi chapters 8 & 9, we learn about the events that happened to the Nephites after the Savior was resurrected. Match the description to it's picture below.

TIMELINE OF EVENTS TO THE RESURRECTED CHRIST VISITING THE NEPHITES

GREAT DOUBTING AMONG PEOPLE THAT CHRIST WOULD COME

GREAT STORM, EARTHQUAKES, FIRES, CITIES SUNK, WICKED DESTROYED

GREAT DARKNESS FOR THREE DAYS

THE PEOPLE HEAR A VOICE THREE TIMES & FINALLY UNDERSTAND IT IS GOD INTRODUCING HIS SON. JESUS CHRIST DESCENDS. THE PEOPLE FEEL HIS NAIL PRINTS.

JESUS TEACHES ABOUT BAPTISM

SEPTEMBER 30-OCTOBER 6

In 3 Nephi 12:14–16, Jesus teaches the people to let their light shine. Below write or draw ways you can let your light shine. Color the candle.

I WILL LET MY LIGHT SHINE

3 NEPHI 12-16

Read 3 Nephi chapter 13. What does Jesus teach about prayer in this chapter?

_____

_____

_____

_____

_____

Read 3 Nephi chapter 14. What does Jesus teach about judging in this chapter?

_____

_____

_____

_____

_____

_____

Read 3 Nephi chapter 15. Who are Jesus' sheep?

_____

_____

_____

_____

_____

Write any notes and/or thoughts about this week's reading below.

_____

_____

_____

_____

_____

_____

OCTOBER 7-13

Read 3 Nephi 17:1-3. Why did Jesus want the people to go home and ponder what He had taught?

_____
_____
_____
_____

Read 3 Nephi 17:11-25. Why did Jesus spend so much time blessing the children? Why did angels minister to the children?

_____
_____
_____
_____

Read 3 Nephi 19:19-36. What did the Savior say in His prayer?

_____
_____
_____
_____
_____

Write any notes and/or thoughts about this week's reading below.

_____
_____
_____
_____
_____
_____
_____
_____

In 3 Nephi 18:1–12, Jesus teaches about the sacrament. Below write what you can think about during the sacrament (scripture, hymn, etc).

I CAN THINK OF JESUS WHEN I TAKE THE SACRAMENT

OCTOBER 14-20

3 Nephi chapter 20. What miracle did Jesus perform at the beginning of this chapter?

_____
_____
_____
_____
_____
_____

Read 3 Nephi 23:6-14. What did Jesus say about the words of Samuel the Lamanite?

_____
_____
_____
_____
_____
_____

Read 3 Nephi chapter 24. Why does God ask us to pay tithing?

_____
_____
_____
_____
_____
_____

Write any notes and/or thoughts about this week's reading below.

_____
_____
_____
_____
_____
_____
_____
_____

3 NEPHI 20-26

In 3 Nephi 25:5–6, we learn about turning "the heart of the fathers to the children" through family history & temple work. Draw a picture of your family below.

FAMILIES CAN BE TOGETHER FOREVER

OCTOBER 21-27

Read 3 Nephi chapter 27. What is the importance of the name of the Savior's church?

_____

_____

_____

_____

_____

Read 4 Nephi 1:1-23. What was it like to live in the years following the Savior's visit?

_____

_____

_____

_____

_____

Read 4 Nephi 1:24-49. What changes occurred in the people to disrupt the happy and peaceful society?

_____

_____

_____

_____

Write any notes and/or thoughts about this week's reading below.

_____

_____

_____

_____

_____

_____

_____

In 3 Nephi 28:1–11, the Savior asks each of His disciples what they desire. Solve the clues below to complete the cross word puzzle.

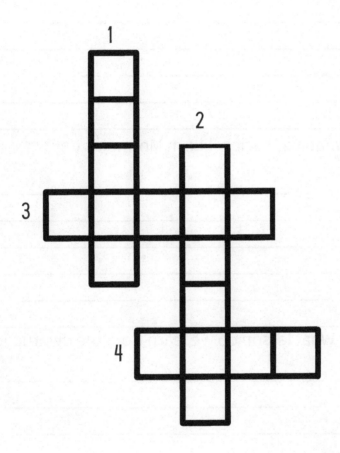

DOWN

1-ALL BUT HOW MANY ASKED FOR THE SAME THING? (VS. 2)

2-JESUS TOLD THESE DISCIPLES WHEN THEY WERE 72 YEARS OLD THEY COULD COME LIVE WITH HIM IN _____

ACROSS

3-THE REMAINING DISCIPLES WISHED TO _____ TASTE DEATH (VS 7)

4-JESUS TOLD THE DISCIPLES THEY WILL COME TO HIS KINGDOM AND FIND_____ (VS 3)

OCTOBER 28-NOVEMBER 3

CIRCLE THE DAYS YOU READ THIS WEEK: MON TUES WED THUR FRI SAT SUN

Read Mormon chapter 1. What do you learn about Mormon? How was he different from his people?

_____

_____

_____

_____

_____

Read Mormon 2:18-19. What was society like in Mormon's day?

_____

_____

_____

_____

_____

Read Mormon chapter 6. What lesson do we learn from the destruction of the Nephites?

_____

_____

_____

_____

_____

Write any notes and/or thoughts about this week's reading below.

_____

_____

_____

_____

_____

_____

_____

MORMON 1-6

In Mormon 3:3, 9, we see the Lord had blessed the Nephites but they were ungrateful. On the leaves below, write or draw what you are grateful for.

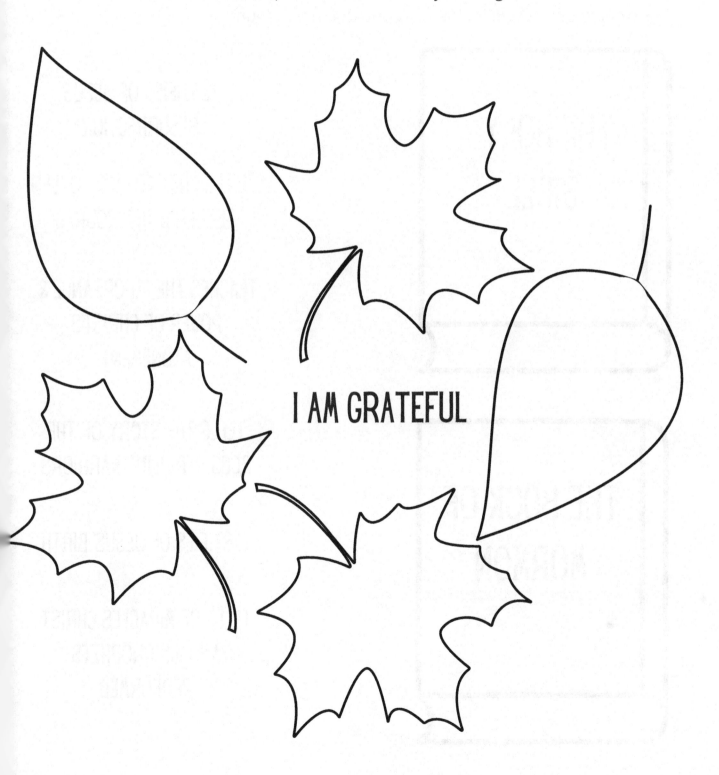

I AM GRATEFUL

NOVEMBER 4-10

In Mormon 7:8–10, we read that the Bible and the Book of Mormon testify of Christ. Read the statements below and draw a line to either the Bible, Book of Mormon or both, depending on where the story and doctrine is found.

THE HOLY BIBLE

THE BOOK OF MORMON

TESTIFIES OF JESUS' RESURRECTION

TELLS THE STORY OF QUEEN ESTHER & HER COURAGE

TEACHES THE IMPORTANCE & POWER OF CHRIST'S ATONEMENT

TELLS THE STORY OF THE 2,000 STRIPLING WARRIORS

TESTIFIES OF JESUS' BIRTH

TELLS OF MIRACLES CHRIST AND HIS PROPHETS PERFORMED

MORMON 7-9

Read Mormon chapter 8. What happened to Mormon? What do we learn about Moroni?

_____

_____

_____

_____

Read Mormon 8:26-41. What did Moroni see in our day?

_____

_____

_____

_____

_____

Read Mormon 9:11-21. What does Moroni say about miracles?

_____

_____

_____

_____

_____

Write any notes and/or thoughts about this week's reading below.

_____

_____

_____

_____

_____

_____

NOVEMBER 11-17

CIRCLE THE DAYS YOU READ THIS WEEK: MON TUES WED THUR FRI SAT SUN

In this week's reading we learn about the Jaredites, who lived at the time of the Tower of Babel. They prayed to the Lord that their language would not be changed so they could still understand each other. The Lord answered their prayer. Color the picture below.

HEAVENLY FATHER HEARS & ANSWERS MY PRAYERS

ETHER 1-5

Read Ether 2:18-23. How can you apply the experience of the brother of Jared to yourself?

_____
_____
_____
_____
_____

Read Ether 3:1-6. What did the brother of Jared do to get light for the barges?

_____
_____
_____
_____
_____

Read Ether 4:12. How do we know if something is of God?

_____
_____
_____
_____
_____

Write any notes and/or thoughts about this week's reading below.

_____
_____
_____
_____
_____
_____
_____

NOVEMBER 18-24

CIRCLE THE DAYS YOU READ THIS WEEK: MON TUES WED THUR FRI SAT SUN

Read Ether chapter 6. How might you compare the Jaredites journey across the sea to your mortal journey?

_____
_____
_____
_____
_____

Read Ether chapter 8. Why was Moroni commanded to write about the secret combinations? (see vs. 26)

_____
_____
_____
_____
_____

Read Ether chapter 9. How do we see the pride cycle in this chapter?

_____
_____
_____
_____
_____

Write any notes and/or thoughts about this week's reading below.

_____
_____
_____
_____
_____
_____
_____

ETHER 6-11

In Ether 6:12, when the Jaredites arrived to the promised land after being on water for 344 days, they shed tears of joy for the "tender mercies" the Lord had showed them. Complete the word search below with words from this week's reading.

```
C  O  M  A  V  G  S  V  J  B  Q
P  F  H  H  S  E  I  C  R  E  M
V  P  J  A  R  E  D  O  S  M  T
P  R  E  D  N  E  T  D  E  M  Q
J  F  R  Q  Y  H  G  S  N  E  Z
P  R  A  Y  E  D  D  E  O  O  N
F  B  E  R  D  S  H  G  T  R  P
Z  L  N  T  L  P  B  R  S  R  U
A  S  A  V  A  B  Q  A  R  E  S
S  T  U  T  H  W  C  B  D  W  M
H  E  I  P  C  G  T  H  G  I  L
```

BROTHER	JARED	BARGES
STONES	LIGHT	PRAYED
WATER	TENDER	MERCIES

NOVEMBER 25-DECEMBER 1

In Ether 12:6, we learn about faith. Complete the verse below with the missing words.

AND NOW, I, _____, WOULD SPEAK SOMEWHAT CONCERNING THESE THINGS; I WOULD SHOW UNTO THE WORLD THAT _____IS THINGS WHICH ARE _____ FOR AND NOT ____; WHEREFORE, DISPUTE NOT BECAUSE YE _____NOT, FOR YE RECEIVE NO WITNESS UNTIL AFTER THE _____OF YOUR FAITH.

ETHER 12-15

Read Ether chapter 12. List some things you learned about Ether in this chapter.

_____

_____

_____

_____

_____

Read Ether chapter 13. What happened to the people when they did not listen to Ether?

_____

_____

_____

_____

_____

Read Ether 15:1-4. Why did Coriantumr finally remember the words Ether had spoken?

_____

_____

_____

_____

_____

Write any notes and/or thoughts about this week's reading below.

_____

_____

_____

_____

_____

_____

_____

DECEMBER 2-8

In Moroni 4:3 and 5:2, we read the sacrament prayers. Can you say these prayers from memory? What are two of the things the prayer asks us to do? Crack the code below to find out.

CRACK THE CODE

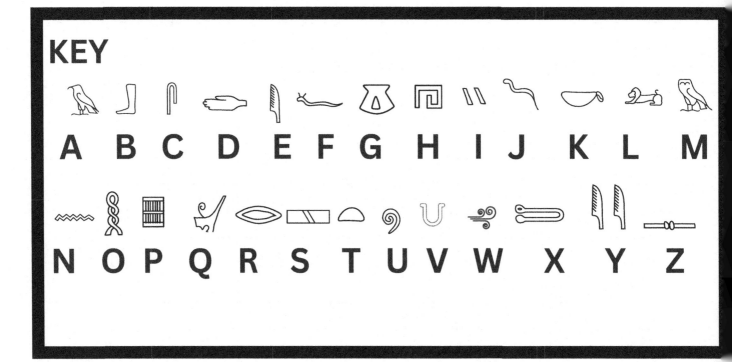

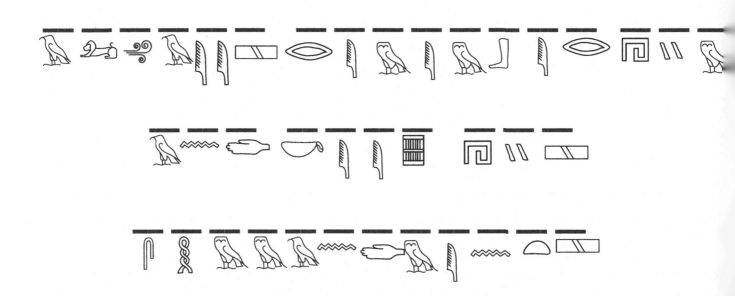

MORONI 1-6

Read Moroni chapter 1. List ways a person could "deny" Christ below.

_____

_____

_____

_____

_____

Read Moroni chapter 2. What do we learn about the ordinance of the confirmation of the Holy Ghost?

_____

_____

_____

_____

_____

Read Moroni chapter 6. What is required to be baptized?

_____

_____

_____

_____

_____

Write any notes and/or thoughts about this week's reading below.

_____

_____

_____

_____

_____

_____

_____

DECEMBER 9-15

Read Moroni 7:12-20. How can we know good from evil?

_____

_____

_____

_____

_____

Read Moroni 8:1-22. What do we learn about the baptism of little children?

_____

_____

_____

_____

_____

Read Moroni 9:22-26. What advice did Mormon give Moroni?

_____

_____

_____

_____

_____

Write any notes and/or thoughts about this week's reading below.

_____

_____

_____

_____

_____

_____

_____

In Moroni 7:47, we read about charity being the pure love of Christ. Think of something kind you can do for someone this week and write or draw what you will do below. Can you think of ways Jesus showed charity?

CHARITY IS THE PURE LOVE OF CHRIST

In Moroni chapter 10, Moroni invites us to ask God if the Book of Mormon is true. Match the phrase below with the correct image.

I CAN ASK GOD IF THE BOOK OF MORMON IS TRUE

MORONI FINISHED WRITING
HIS RECORD

MORONI INVITES US TO READ
THE BOOK OF MORMON

ONCE WE READ THE BOOK OF
MORMON, WE SHOULD ASK
GOD IF IT IS TRUE

IF WE ASK WITH FAITH, HOLY
GHOST WILL LET US KNOW
THE RECORD IS TRUE

MORONI BURIED THE PLATES.
HIS MORTAL WORK WAS
FINISHED.

MORONI 10

Read Moroni 10:3-5. What is the promise of the Book of Mormon? Have you prayed with "real intent"?

_____
_____
_____
_____

Read Moroni 10:8-17. What spiritual gifts do you have?

_____
_____
_____
_____
_____

Read Moroni 10:20-23. How are hope, faith, and charity connected?

_____
_____
_____
_____
_____

Write any notes and/or thoughts about this week's reading below.

_____
_____
_____
_____
_____
_____
_____

DECEMBER 23-29

The Book of Mormon testifies of Jesus Christ, as stated in 2 Nephi 25:23. Reflect on all you have learned this year & write about or draw your favorite scripture story or favorite person from the Book of Mormon below.

THE BOOK OF MORMON TESTIFIES OF CHRIST

CHRISTMAS

Read 1 Nephi 11:13-36. What impressions come to you after reading these verses?

_____

_____

_____

_____

_____

Read Helaman 14:1-13. What signs were to be given at Christ's birth?

_____

_____

_____

_____

_____

Read 1 Nephi 6:4; 19:18; and 2 Nephi 25:23, 26; 33:4, 10. How does the Book of Mormon testify of Jesus Christ?

_____

_____

_____

_____

Write any notes and/or thoughts about this week's reading below.

_____

_____

_____

_____

_____

_____

_____

GOAL REFLECTION

How did you do with your spiritual, physical, social, and intellectual goals this past year? Write about each goal below.

_____
_____
_____
_____
_____
_____
_____
_____
_____
_____
_____
_____

In space below, write your testimony and what you have learned from studying the Book of Mormon this year.

_____
_____
_____
_____
_____
_____
_____
_____
_____
_____
_____
_____

IF YOU ENJOYED THIS BOOK, MAKE SURE TO LEAVE A REVIEW.

CHECK OUT OUR OTHER BOOKS.

FOLLOW US ONLINE!

@LATTER.DAY.DESIGNS

LATTER-DAY DESIGNS

Made in the USA
Las Vegas, NV
07 January 2024

84008296R00063